IN CHARGE
Issue nº 18 — Summer 2022

PART 1

On the cover, photographer Davey Adésida captures the
immeasurable energy of DIANE VON FURSTENBERG.

PART 2

The Book of the Season, Nella Larsen's novel PASSING,
prompts stories on race, code-switching and the whirlwind
of Harlem in the 1920s.

Design by Harlem Renaissance artist
Aaron Douglas for a 1927 issue of The Crisis
magazine, the official publication of the
National Association for the Advancement
of Colored People (NAACP).

A work entitled *Book* (2019) by British conceptual artist MICHAEL CRAIG-MARTIN. As an everyday object rendered in a bright colour palette, *Book* belongs to a long-running thread in Craig-Martin's practice also including a *Trumpet* (2019), some *Sunglasses* (2016) and a table *Fan* (1993).

AURA

Although the shop is narrow, it is possible, if for example you are by Science Fiction and wish to access Self-help, to pass by another customer. They will need to be facing sideways and so will you, and if they are looking at a shelf it will be necessary for them to step a little closer to it. Backpacks were hopefully left by the counter, as requested on the sign. If passer and passee are facing one another, the passer may smile but shouldn't make eye contact. The passee should act as if nobody's there.

It'd be less tense if it weren't for a quietness generated by a tendency to mistake bookshops for libraries. It'd be less awkward if it weren't for the subtext of having something in common: whether web developers or bus drivers, we're all happy readers here. By comparison there's no implied shared interest between you and the stranger in the supermarket, even if, for purely practical reasons, you'd rather be trapped in a supermarket than a bookshop.

A book bought from a bookshop has a special aura. Not a magic one. It's not a New Age store. More a glow of association brought about by the memory of having gone somewhere fascinating to acquire it, one of those places that are filled, as Martin Latham puts it in his memoir *The Bookseller's Tale*, with 'a sense of immanence, of being on the verge of infinite inner space'.

THE HAPPY READER — Bookish Magazine — Issue n° 18
The Happy Reader is a collaboration between Penguin Books and Fantastic Man

EDITOR-IN-CHIEF Seb Emina ART DIRECTOR Matthew Young MANAGING EDITOR Maria Bedford EDITORIAL DIRECTORS Jop van Bennekom, Gert Jonkers PICTURE RESEARCH Frances Roper PRODUCTION Katy Banyard MARKETING Liz Parsons BRAND DIRECTOR Sam Voulters MARKETING DIRECTOR Ingrid Matts PUBLISHER Stefan McGrath CONTRIBUTORS Davey Adésida, Gabrielle Bellot, Wayde Compton, Michael Craig-Martin, Awol Erizku, Nathaniel Feldmann, Morgan Jerkins, Jordan Kelly, Roisin Kiberd, Georgina Lawton, Willy Ndatira, Rob Palk, Lorna Simpson THANK YOU Michael Famighetti, Paul Flynn, Alexander Hurst, Hilal Isler, Olga Kominek, Rebecca Lee, Penny Martin, Richard O'Mahony, Casey Murphy, Aaron Peck, Rosa Rankin-Gee, Ilaria Rovera, Anna Wilson

PENGUIN BOOKS 20 Vauxhall Bridge Road London SW1V 2SA info@thehappyreader.com www.thehappyreader.com

SNIPPETS

Stories of book-love featuring actors,
pop stars and library enthusiasts

BOOK + SKIN   A trio of literary tattoos on celebrity arms: Angelina Jolie has a line from the Tennessee Williams play *Stairs to the Roof*; Ryan Gosling has an image from a children's book, *The Giving Tree*; and Lady Gaga has a quote from Rilke's *Letters to a Young Poet*. That last one's written in the original German and translates as: 'Look deep into your heart, where it spreads its roots, for the answer: can you avow that you would die if you were forbidden to write? Must I write?'

DAIRY FANTASY

This year's Venice Biennale, which is in fact the postponed 2021 edition of the contemporary art extravaganza, is entitled *The Milk of Dreams*. Why so? The title, explains curator Cecilia Alemani, is taken from that of a children's book by Leonora Carrington, 'in which the Surrealist artist describes a magical world where life is constantly re-envisioned through the prism of the imagination'. To which the pedant might reply: 'Well, so what? Isn't that just "the world"?' To which the British-born Mexican artist Carrington, whose fans include Björk and whose other books include *The Hearing Trumpet*, about a sinister retirement home, might say, were she still alive: 'I don't know, does your sofa eat vitamins? Do you know someone whose head has turned into a house?'

APE SHAPE

Real things overheard in bookshops: (1) 'I've got to have this! It's so out-of-date it's fantastic.' (2) 'I love the sun back home, but here it's just a decoration.' (3) 'We're primates. I'm just trying to live in accord with what the primatologists have established.'

TIME FOR PROUST

It's the centenary of the death of Marcel Proust, the radical dandy whose seven-novel series *In Search of Lost Time* is something every serious reader must grapple with at least once. Paris is duly filled with exhibitions about his life and work, such as a focus on his Jewishness (*Marcel Proust: On His Mother's Side*, at the Museum of the Art and History of Judaism), and another offering a volume-by-volume journey through the novels (*Marcel Proust: The Factory of Work*, at the National Library), including that ludicrously long dinner party in Book 3, my God.

BORROWING BATTLE

When their local library was billed for closure, residents of a town in England fought back with the literary equivalent of a bank run, checking out every last one of its 16,000 books. Each card holder had a personal allocation of fifteen titles, and each claimed that allocation in full, thus leaving the shelves in Stony Stratford Library, Milton Keynes, embarrassingly bare. The council, now outflanked, changed its mind.

PROM

American actor Nicolas Cage revealed his favourite fictional character to be Dmitri Karamazov, the hedonistic elder brother from Fyodor Dostoyevsky's *The Brothers Karamazov*. During an AMA (Ask Me Anything) session on Reddit, he explained: 'I love him so much because he's so happy and he has no money. He's just living it up. He spent all his money trying to get the girl. I was very Dmitri Karamazov in high school. The most beautiful girl who was a grade older than me invited me to the prom but I had no money. My grandmother gave each of us a little bond. My older brother bought a car. My second oldest brother bought some stereo equipment. And I splashed out on a chauffeur-driven limousine, a tuxedo and a four-course meal at Le Dome on Sunset Blvd. The car was $2000, the stereo was $2000, and my prom night was $2000 and man, that was money well spent. THAT's Dmitri Karamazov.'

BOOKY LOOK

An essay by style writer Derek Guy identified what is now recognised as a key luxury trend for 2022. 'Many people considered cool in the online fashion community dress like the people I see at my local bookstore,' he wrote on his blog *Die Workwear*. He calls this tendency 'bookcore' and defines it as 'an amalgamation of the last five years of trends: normcore, gorpcore, dadcore, vintage, 1990s sportswear, American trad, Westernwear, Native American jewellery, pleats, dad caps, wide-legged trousers, oversized eyewear, Balmacaans, leather blazers, Patagonia, chunky sneakers, intentionally ugly shoes, etc'.

GROWTH SPURT

When an author finishes the process of writing a book they often feel in some way changed. Few, however, have experienced a transformation like Mieko Kawakami, Japanese author of the novel *Heaven*, who told the Booker Prize website that, 'when I was done writing it, I was three centimetres taller'.

HOARDER

Happy Reader alumnus Jarvis Cocker offers a new solution for dealing with one's childhood junk: bookify it. The singer's new memoir, *Good Pop, Bad Pop*, takes the form of an inventory of all the old crap in his London loft. Objects unearthed include a twenty-year-old pack of chewing gum and a magazine called *The Fantastic Dirty Joke Book*. Write it up then throw it out... Everyone needs to do this!

HOLY WETSHIRT

Remember 1995's television adaptation of *Pride and Prejudice* where Mr Darcy, played by Colin Firth, emerges from a lake wearing a white shirt clinging suggestively to his torso? That shirt has, it seems, been preserved for veneration. It has now washed up in an exhibition at Jane Austen's House, a museum in the English village of Chawton. The rest of the show is called *Jane Austen Undressed* and focuses on the hypothetical underwear of Jane Austen's characters. It is on until 2 October.

SHE DID WHAT!

Actress Ashley Tisdale sparked outrage by revealing how, before a photoshoot for *Architectural Digest*, she sent her husband to purchase 400 books to fill a set of bookshelves in her Los Angeles home. Her defence: a lot of people plump up their libraries for such shoots but 'I was just honest about it.' The hastily gathered selection included Elton John's *Me* and a book called *Salt Block Cooking* by Mark Bitterman.

DIANE VON FURSTE

Interview by
SEB EMINA

Portraits by
DAVEY ADÉSIDA

ERG Reading, writing, publishing, collecting.
Dispatches from the library of fashion's No.1 royalty.

PARIS

Diane von Furstenberg's Paris apartment is in the very literary neighbourhood of Saint-Germain-des-Prés. It's a place where a third of thrown stones hit bookshops so beautiful it feels taboo to go into them, another third hit cafes once frequented by famous authors, and a final third hit booksellers based out of the dark green riverside stands called *bouquinistes*. These latter also do a roaring trade in vintage fashion magazines, and it's a safe bet that on any given day it will be possible to find at least one with Diane herself on the cover.

This is not Diane's main residence. The capacious home she shares with her husband, the media executive Barry Diller, is in Connecticut. Her six-storey HQ is in Manhattan's Meatpacking District. But she has lived in Paris on more than one occasion, and retains strong ties to the city. Two years ago the French government named her a *Chevalier de la Légion d'Honneur*.

She gestures for me to sit in an armchair by a coffee table on which are arranged issues of *National Geographic* and *New York* magazines and a large-format photo book about the Statue of Liberty, the museum of which she once raised $100 million for. She pours me a cup of ginger tea then disappears into an adjacent room for a moment to switch off a TV or radio relaying news of the situation in Ukraine.

It is a formidable experience, being in the room with Diane von Furstenberg, who launched her career in 1974 with the invention of the wrap dress, a staple for women's wardrobes so instantly ubiquitous that it was a little like inventing risotto, or rock music, or the deckchair. That dress sold a million units in two years and saw her propelled to the very top of the celebrity firmament. *Newsweek* described her in an early cover story as 'the most marketable woman since Coco Chanel'.

She is fashion royalty, then, but she's also *royalty* royalty: an actual princess (or, strictly speaking, an ex-princess, though some

auras never dissipate). Having been born with the surname Halfin in Brussels in 1946, Diane went on to marry Egon von Fürstenberg, a socialite, banker and prince. They had two children together then separated amicably, finally divorcing in 1983.

Diane is sometimes referred to simply as DVF, which is also the name of the fashion house she built up in the 1970s, gave up for a time in the 1980s, before relaunching it in the late 1990s as the wrap dress exploded back into fashion. Other business ventures have included perfume brands, jewellery, beachwear and a line of children's clothes for GapKids. From 2006 to 2019 she was chairwoman of the Council of Fashion Designers of America. In 2014, Forbes named her the 68th most powerful woman in the world.

Her passion for seizing all of life's potential is in part the legacy of a Jewish mother who was involved with the Belgian Resistance before being sent to Auschwitz in 1944. There's a story Diane often tells, which has acquired the status of a foundational legend. It's about how her mother made friends with an older woman on the train to the camp, how new arrivals were then directed into two groups, and how the woman from the train was sent to the left and Diane's mother tried to follow, only to be violently pushed into the group on the right by a white-coated officer. 'My mother always said that she'd never felt such sheer hatred for anyone as she felt for that man,' writes Diane in her memoir, *The Woman I Wanted to Be*. Except he saved her life: 'The group the older woman was assigned to went directly to the gas chamber.' The man, it turned out, was the notorious Dr Josef Mengele, nicknamed 'the Angel of Death' for his brutal experiments on prisoners. His reasons for saving her are forever unknown.

Despite her strong association with New York, Diane's accent is elusively European. This may be something to do with her father's Moldovan background or, more likely, what she calls her 'crazy life', travelling all over the place as her fancies dictate. Indeed, she is on the phone at her house in the Bahamas when we talk again a week later — in a conversation I have combined with the one below.

Sitting on her Paris sofa, she often slips into French as she speaks. At other times she slips into another room altogether, looking for some artefact or volume that will elucidate a point she is making, shouting her answer to my previous question as she rummages through a drawer or box. As we start, she asks me a few questions about myself, then, with a certain business-like zeal, launches straight into the subject we have agreed to discuss.

DIANE: Books have been very, very, very important in my life. Always. I never played with dolls. I loved books even before I could read. I knew them by heart, so I used to pretend I knew when to turn the page. I had these little children's books, I forget what they were called in French, but I never knew which book to choose so I always carried a stack of them from room to room. And the funny thing is, I still do that. I am still that little girl with a stack of books.

SEB: Did that make you want to be a writer or to create books in some way? Or did you always want to be a fashion designer?

D: When people asked me, 'What do you want to be?' I didn't know exactly, but I knew the kind of woman I wanted to be. I wanted to be a woman in charge. I wanted to be free. But how would I get there? I didn't know, so I said, 'What can you do if you like books?' And the person I asked, I don't remember who it was, they could have said, 'You could be a writer,' and instead they said, 'Oh, you could be a librarian.' The librarian at my school was this horrible person with very thick glasses and bad breath, and the idea of being that person was absolutely not what I had in mind. But books, they'd take you places. It was a sense of adventure. Through books, I could go anywhere and I loved that. I did write my diary, though, very early on. I've written my diary all my life.

S: I read somewhere you have archives containing thousands of your old diaries. Do you go back and look through them often?

D: No. Only occasionally, if I need a reference or something, like when I was writing my book. Then of course I wanted to read again when I had cancer, things like that. They're not always that interesting, but what is important about writing your diary is that you have a communion with yourself. A communion with yourself is the most important thing you can do, and that's my advice to everyone... I mean, I cannot tell you the amount of diaries that I've bought for people, including little children.

S: Do you always buy people the same one? Is there a model of diary you swear by?

D: Well, a Smythson or Hermès. I mean, I buy nice ones.

S: What did you read as you grew older?

D: I read a lot of novels, a lot of French literature. Guy de Maupassant and Émile Zola and Balzac. *La Chartreuse de Parme* [*The Charterhouse of Parma*] by Stendhal. Flaubert. I mean, books like that. And *Le Grand Meaulnes*. If I were to give you my favourite book of all time, it's probably *Le Petit Prince* [*The Little Prince*].

S: Why that book above all others?

D: Because it is so simple and so full of symbols. Because it's

'My favourite writer,
I think it is Stefan Zweig.'

philosophy. You remember, he had a small planet. It was so small that all he had to do was push his chair a little bit and he would see a sunset all day, and then he met the businessman who was counting money all the time, and then he met the drunkard, and he said:

1. PLANE CRASH
—
Antoine de Saint-Exupéry and his navigator crashed in the Sahara Desert on 30 December 1935 during participation in a Paris-to-Saigon air race.

'Pourquoi tu bois?'
'Je bois pour oublier.'
'Pour oublier quoi?'

['Why do you drink?'
'I drink to forget.'
'To forget what?']

You know, all the symbols. He was in love with the rose and she was so capricious, and she needed some protection. Everything is in that book, *mais ceci dit, je ne suis pas sure qu'il était tellement sympathique, Saint-Exupéry* [but that said, I'm not sure if he was very likeable, Saint-Exupéry].

S: I remember finding Saint-Exupéry's life story incredible though. The fact he was really in a plane crash and then lost in the Sahara, just these two completely impossible situations, one after the other, and lived to talk about it... Have you read his other books? Have you read *Wind, Sand and Stars*?

D: I tried a long time ago, but then I wasn't into it. There's an exhibition in Paris. You should go. The only thing I've done here, other than seeing three friends, is go to the bookstore, and there was a beautiful book on Saint-Exupéry. I almost bought it. It's explaining all the drawings, everything like that, and it says it's from an exhibition at the Musée des Arts Décoratifs.

S: So he's not your favourite writer.

D: My favourite writer, I was thinking about it this morning. I think it is Stefan Zweig. I have read every Stefan Zweig book. I just bought three little Stefan Zweigs this morning. He was so brilliant. I like the detachment, but of course he had a terrible end. He wrote all these great biographies, the best book on Marie Antoinette. Did you ever read that? On Magellan, and, of course, *Farewell to Europe*, which is what he wrote before he killed himself. But then, of course, I love the Russians as well. Dostoyevsky and Tolstoy and Turgenev and *Oblomov*. I don't remember who wrote *Oblomov*. Did you ever read *Oblomov*? Do you know what it is?

S: I don't know *Oblomov*.

D: I just downloaded it. Oblomov is a man who is very, very lazy. And the whole book is describing how he stays in bed. That's the entire book, and it takes him three hours just to turn.

S: That's a very Russian story.

D: I also love *Mitteleuropa* literature such as Kafka and Canetti and Joseph Roth. My favourites are probably those and South American books.

S: As in, Borges? Gabriel García Márquez?

D: Gabriel García Márquez, Borges, Onetti, Manuel Puig, especially Puig. I love his writing. I love the way he describes women. There's a book by him called *Boquitas Pintadas* [*Heartbreak Tango*]. It's fantastic. Also Ernesto Sabato, *The Tunnel*, all of that. I went to Argentina and I met Ernesto Sabato before he died, and I also met Bioy Casares, who wrote with Borges. I don't know if it's Borges or Casares who had a family that made yoghurt and started out by writing copy for yoghurt.

S: I had no idea! There's a lot of money in yoghurt, I guess.

D: I think it was yoghurt. Definitely dairy.

S: You mentioned something about writing your book earlier. I assume you meant your memoir. One story that really moved me when I read it was about your mother, about the moment when the Nazis arrested her in Brussels, and they put her in a truck, and she wrote a letter addressed to her parents and threw it out onto the street. How she just hoped it would be found by someone who'd take it to them.

D: I have the letter. I have it. When she used to tell me the story, I'd say, 'Yeah, yeah.' I didn't ever believe it. And then I found it.

S: So her parents, or your grandparents, they had it all along?

D: Yes. They got it. I mean, it was written, and addressed to her parents, and it was delivered. But she did not know that her parents got it because when she survived and she arrived home, the people who arrived from the camp, nobody wanted to talk about it. So you didn't talk about it. You didn't think about it. But her older sister kept it. And when my mother died and I lent my house in Harbor Island to my cousin, he left for me a shoebox full of photographs. And most of the photographs I had seen, but underneath there was an envelope that was so flat because it had been flat for sixty years. And I opened it, and there were these two notes. I could not believe it. I was shaking. I couldn't believe it. And she says to her mother, '*Je ne sais pas ou je vais, mais sachez que je pars avec le sourire*' ['I don't know where I'm

2. YOGHURT
—

Jorge Luis Borges and Bioy Casares' brochure for Argentinian yoghurt brand La Martona was published in 1936 with the title *La leche cuajada de La Martona* (La Martona's Yoghurt).

going, but I want you to know that I'm leaving with a smile']. And I went, because my mother, her house is by the sea, by the beautiful beach and by the sea, and I went down there and I said, 'This is exactly who I am. I am the daughter of someone who went to the camps with a smile.'

S: What comes through in your book is the existence of and importance of letters. Handwritten letters, typed letters... a physical record of what's gone before. That was a big example but not the only one.

   D: I have letters, I write letters. I wrote to my children. They think I'm a bad mother, but I wrote to them every single day while they were in school or camp.

S: Do you still write to them?

   D: I do, every birthday. I make a drawing and I write a big letter. And not only do I write, but my poor children and grandchildren at Christmas and New Years, for my birthday — everyone has to write me a letter.

S: So what's in your stack of books right now?

   D: Well, I now read on Audible a lot. Audible is a dream because I can do jigsaw puzzles. I have an addiction, which is doing jigsaw puzzles with my own photographs. Here, you see?

   [*She shows me the screen of her iPad, on which a picture has been scrambled into a digital jigsaw.*]

That's an example. I mean, this is my photograph, and I make it into a jigsaw puzzle.

S: There's an app that does this?

   D: Yes. It's very relaxing, it's very good for your brain, but you waste so much time. Somehow, now, I discovered that I can do that while I'm listening to an audiobook because it's two parts of my brain that are not connected.

S: Have you played Wordle?

   D: No. I don't want to. I know about it, and I don't want to touch it. OK. Now we go to Audible. You can see I have a lot of books on Venetians. I am obsessed with Venice at the moment. I have this big project that I want to do.

S: You were in Venice this week, weren't you?

   D: Yes, and that's why. I've gone to Venice, I think, for just a few

1.

2.

6.

News TIONAL NEWSMAGAZINE
Rags & Riches **week**

May 3, 1976

Dress
Designer
Diane von
Fürstenberg

7.

5.

10.

9.

Alex Majoli Magnum Photos

Photo Susan Wood / Getty Images

© Alex Majoli Magnum Photos

8.

© Elliott Erwitt Magnum Photos

11.

4.

1. Holding a yoga pose in 1977. 2. Scrutinising a garment in 2009. 3. Details from a pair of dresses in 2009. 4. Talking business on the phone in 1982. 5. Leafing through a hardback in 1976. 6. In a wrap dress on the cover of *Newsweek* in 1976. 7. Detail from a patterned fabric in 2009. 8. On a plane at JFK airport in 1979. 9. In the studio in 1991 showing her collection for spring 1992. 10. In a car when it's raining in 1976. 11. With first husband Prince Egon von Fürstenberg in 1970.

days every single year since I was seventeen. The first time was with my father and my brother. Then when I started going out with Egon, who became my husband; his mother lived outside Venice and was very involved in the city. Later, I would go to these balls in Venice. I went to Venice with every man of my life. I've gone many, many times but it has recently taken a much bigger role in my imagination.

S: Because of this project?

D: Yes. I am reading many, many, many books on the history of Venice because I'm fascinated by what she is, and I say 'she' because one of my dreams, and something that I am starting to incubate, is to write a history of Venice in the first person but with her being a woman, because I've never wanted to be any woman other than myself, but I would like to be Venice. Venice is 1,500 years of history, and so many things started there. Venice invented bureaucracy and customs and diplomacy. It was the end of the Silk Road. It was where art and commerce met. Every painter went to Venice; every writer wrote about Venice. To me, she is really the epitome of a seductress.

S: I read Jan Morris's Venice book years ago and the detail that stuck with me for some reason was the *bocche dei lioni* from the Venetian Empire, little postboxes resembling lions' heads where you could just anonymously denounce people to the authorities. I think you can still see them, if you know where to look. Do you know Jan Morris's book?

D: Which one is that? No, tell me the name.

S: It's just called *Venice*. I remember the first time I went there I read that at the same time and was completely spellbound by it.

D: From now on please send me anything you see on Venice that I should read.

S: I definitely will. I often also think about how I'd love to watch a lavish prestige TV series about Venice.

D: A documentary. That's my secret next project. A documentary, and therefore first a book, telling the story of Venice. Hopefully I will be able to achieve that before I die.

S: Do you have a favourite Venice book so far?

D: Professor Madden, a historian from St Louis... I really like his book. But I'm reading all kinds, anything I can find, trivial or not.

[*She looks through the titles on her iPad.*]

Life with Picasso, I'm reading that... Then something about Jung...

Then this one I haven't read yet, *The Artist, the Philosopher and the Warrior*. Somebody must have recommended this... Then one about Karl Lagerfeld... *The Hidden Life of Trees*...

S: That's meant to be amazing.

D: Is it? I haven't read it yet. *Identity* by Fukuyama... *Empire of Pain*? I don't even know what that is... *The Chancellor* I read, the biography of Angela Merkel. Very interesting... Something on Man Ray... Leïla Slimani... And I read Huma Abedin's autobiography... *The Will to Meaning*, that's Viktor Frankl... *Les Mémoires d'Hadrien* [*Memoirs of Hadrian*], Yourcenar... Nietzsche... Here, *Putin v. the People*... But I'm only about halfway.

S: Do you finish one and then carry on to the next one? Or just kind of jump around?

D: Well, sometimes I interrupt, but you get a sense. Gandhi's autobiography, *The Story of My Experiments with Truth*... *La Peste* [*The Plague*], Albert Camus. When Covid started I reread that... *The History of Philosophy*... Karl Marx... Hitler... Simon Schama, *Citizens*... And then I read four huge tomes of Napoleon... *Silk Road*... *The Ottomans*... Then George Sand — somebody talked to me about her again, so I wanted to read that... *The Autobiography of Malcolm X*... *Believing* by Anita Hill... *Yes to Life*, another book by Viktor Frankl...

S: At the beginning of your memoir, you say that it was thanks to your mother that you're an avid reader. What did you read together?

D: Oh, well, with her I read a lot of encyclopedias. At the time, the Larousse had this little dictionary, and on the first page there were drawings suggesting words that began with different letters of the alphabet, and you had to guess the word.

S: So you would sit together, playing this game?

D: Yes, and that's so weird that you mentioned that, because actually it works. Somehow, I do that now. I never thought about that before. I mean, I remember, but I never associated it with... Oh, you know what I'm going to do? I'm going to read you my introduction. I'll explain. I wrote this book during Covid because a publisher came to me and said, 'You know, people quote you all the time. You have all these pieces of wisdom, and we do so well with these feel-good books, and we would like to have a book called *In Charge*.'

S: As in, the kind of woman you wanted to be when you grew up?

D: Yes, but then also, later, when people would ask me, 'Who do you dress?' I would say, 'The woman in charge.' The woman in

3. KARL LAGERFELD
—
Last year's Sotheby's auction dedicated to the late fashion designer's belongings included a black, relacquered wooden step ladder with which Lagerfeld had accessed the higher volumes from his vast collection of books. Originally estimated to fetch between €2,000 and €3,000, the item eventually sold for €22,680.

'My choice in literature
has always been about
strong women.'

charge was somehow always this umbrella over my life. A few years ago I wrote a little manifesto about it. Being in charge is not aggressive, it's a commitment to yourself. It's owning who you are, owning your imperfections. You own your vulnerability if you turn it into strengths, right? Anyway, they wanted me to write a book about that, and first of all I didn't want to call it *In Charge*, because if you see that as a title, it's kind of arrogant. Then I started to write it as prose and it sounded so condescending and so annoying that I wrote it like a dictionary. I picked words from each letter of the alphabet.

S: Ah right, like the Larousse game!

D: Yes. Each time it's either a definition or an anecdote. For example, 'connect'. Every morning I try to make one miracle, and the miracle is about connecting people to either another person or to things. Or 'expand', which means expanding your horizon. My advice is, at least once a week, to try to give quality time to someone that you normally wouldn't do that with. You think you do it for them, and of course you do, but you also do it for you, because in doing so you expand your universe.

S: So it's a kind of symbiosis.

D: Yes, like when my friends get fired, or have a big problem, or a bad article is written about them, I call and I say, 'Listen, these things that right now are the worst things, remember them. Because when, twenty years from now, you do your TED talk or write a book, those details are the best anecdotes and the most inspiring stories.' If you tell people that, they look at it in a different way. I have a friend. Every time he had a bad article, and he had a lot because he was running a big department store that was going into bankruptcy, he said he had a beautiful box that his grandmother gave him, and every bad article he would put in that box and it changed the whole perspective.

S: Do you enjoy writing?

D: I love words. Words are extremely powerful. I mean, people use words so ridiculously, without thinking, like people say, 'Oh, I would die.' No, you won't die. I mean, why are you saying that? Words have energy, and you have to be very careful how you use them. And because they have energy, they can make things happen. And so this is now the new one, *Live It: The Secret to Joy*.

[*She goes into another room and returns with a ring-bound notepad. It is filled with handwritten text. On certain pages are mounted clipped-out images of lush ferns.*]

23

S: So this is the manuscript?

D: Yes. The photos are important. I think it's better if I read it from here, because I think that's where I corrected it:

A while back, I had to do a full medical scan of my body, and as I was lying still on the table, trying to occupy my mind, I had a crazy idea. What if they took an X-ray of my soul? What image would come, emerge? That question stayed with me for months. I always knew that my birth had been a victory. Eleven months before I was conceived, my mother, liberated from the death camps, was just a skeleton amongst ashes. Her survival was miraculous, and so was my birth. I always took great pride in the fact that my mother had turned misery into triumph, and that defined who I was. After months of thinking about what the visual of my soul could be, a clear image appeared. I am a fiddlehead, a straight, strong, solitary shoot of green with a curly hand that slowly but surely unfolded into a large leaf with endless possibilities. I've always loved ferns, the most ancient of plants. And it makes total sense that this is how I feel and see life. Life is magic. Life is will. Life is a miracle, and to live it is the secret to joy. To live it is to seize and embrace the moment. It is diving into the present, honouring it, however difficult it may be. To live it is being grateful, being aware, taking responsibility, being engaged and conscious, but also being able to practise detachment. Our life is our journey, our commitment, our strength and our companion. Life makes us part of humanity. So with this little book, I invite you to reflect on all the manifestations of life, to honour it, enjoy it and design it.

S: That's beautiful.

D: It's out in September. I'm very late with it. But when you write, so much is about the incubation.

[*She stands up to return the manuscript.*]

S: Is this the same flat you moved into in 1980 or so?

D: No. I was in number 12, and it was a much grander apartment with very high ceilings. It was a rental, and then after many years they kicked me out, so I bought this. It's very cosy.

S: Didn't you once have your own publishing house in France?

D: I have some of the books here, but other than *American Psycho*, which I brought, I wasn't really that involved. But I did bring *American Psycho*.

S: Wait, you were behind the first French edition of *American Psycho*?

D: Yeah, and it's so funny, La Hune [French bookshop] had it upside down in the window. So I went there, and I didn't say I was the publisher. I said, 'Why is the book upside down?' And he said, 'Because the writer is upside down.' It was very violent. People took that book very violently.

S: Did it do well here?

D: I don't know, because the guy that I helped finance that was, I don't know... But the books were beautiful. Have you seen the books?

[*She gets up and walks into an adjacent room lined with bookshelves, and then calls for me to follow her.*]

He looked at books as beautiful objects, but he was a little pedantic himself, you know. It's not totally my taste. It's all translated. It's good, but... Here's one.

[*She hands me a copy of the first French edition of* American Psycho.]

I only have two, so I can't give it to you. But you can have this one.

[*She gives me a French edition of* My Father and Myself *by J. R. Ackerley, then starts looking at other titles on the bookshelf we are facing.*]

Henri Troyat was a French writer. I don't know if you know anything about him.

S: No, I don't know him.

D: He was very... When I was a little girl, he used to write a lot of books episode by episode, because all the Russian novels would be serialised in the newspaper. They were like *feuilletons*, you know what I mean? And he lived here. I went to meet him with Alain, who was a writer himself — he has a French name, but he's an Italian writer. Those five years that I lived with Alain Elkann in Paris, that was when I fulfilled the fantasy of being a muse to a writer and having a literary salon. I mean, Alberto Moravia lived with us the last two years of his life with his son. He had always been my favourite writer. Bernard-Henri Lévy was a very close friend. And we visited Troyat in his apartment right next door on rue Bonaparte. This is someone that I read when I was a teenage girl, so I was very impressed.

S: What did he look like?

D: He looked like a lion. In fact, another writer who I loved when

4. RUE BONAPARTE
—
Pleasingly, this is just round the corner from a street named rue de Furstemberg, which is actually named after Prince Wilhelm Egon von Fürstenberg-Heiligenberg, an early member of Diane's first husband's house. Forget the errant 'm': spellings were less fixed in 1697, when the prince was appointed abbot of Saint-Germain-des-Prés.

Diane is photographed not in Paris but New
Milton, Connecticut, at the 100-acre property
she shares with her husband, Barry Diller.

I was a teenage girl and then met later on was Joseph Kessel, and he really looked like a lion. Actually he wrote a very famous book called *The Lion*.

S: When you say that he looked like a lion, do you mean that he had lustrous locks of hair or more that he had a sort of bearing of pride and ferocity?

D: I mean really physically like a lion, with a big head and... I don't know, the force, the strength. He also wrote a book about a doctor, I forget the name, but it's the story of Himmler's masseur. It's fantastic.

[She turns back to the bookshelves.]

This is one of the best books ever on Tolstoy. It's an Italian guy who wrote it, Alberto Cavallari. *La Fuga di Tolstoj.* It's about the last week of Tolstoy's life when he runs away. He runs away from his wife and dies in the station. Oh, God. Arthur Miller. I met him.

S: I can't believe I'm talking to someone who actually met Arthur Miller. What was he like?

D: He was just exactly the way you would have expected. I think I met him through Bill Styron, but I did go to his house. He and Inge, he was married to the photographer Inge, who was the mother of Rebecca Miller. These are all neighbours in Connecticut. So these were all neighbourly interactions.

S: You had a drink or a dinner with him? How did it work?

D: I don't remember, but I did go to their house a few times. So I guess I had dinner there.

S: In your career as a fashion designer, has your love of books fed into the products you've created at all, whether directly or indirectly?

D: Well, my choice in literature has always been about strong women. The two things that influence me most, the two threads that have never been interrupted, are the strength of women and the endless inspiration of nature. I discovered nature when I was at boarding school in England, and that's the same time that I discovered the poetry of John Keats. 'A thing of beauty is a joy for ever.'

[She turns to a different shelf.]

OK, so these are all books from my childhood. *Doctor Zhivago* by

5. PHOTOGRAPHER INGE
—
This is the famed photographer Inge Morath, to whom Arthur Miller was married for forty years. He had previously been married to Mary Grace Slattery (fifteen years) and Marilyn Monroe (five).

Boris Pasternak. Why are these books here? I don't know where they came from.

S: I watched a documentary about you, I think it was made by Arte, where Salman Rushdie shows up in the audience of one of your shows. Have you sometimes tried to nurture a literary circle around your work, your brand?

D: Well, it's not around my brand, it's around me, as friends. I've always been attracted by writers and I have gone out of my way to meet them. Salman Rushdie is one. Jerzy Kosiński, I remember as a young girl I read *The Painted Bird* and then he became my friend, as did Bill Styron, who was my neighbour in the country. So was Philip Roth, though unfortunately he was just an acquaintance, not really a friend... *L'Idiot* [*The Idiot*]. Oh my God, my son! When my children were teenagers, I gave my daughter all the lesbian books. All these wonderful lesbian women in Paris. You know, like Natalie Barney. And my son, I gave him *The Idiot*, the Dostoyevsky, and he did not take this well at all. He thought that I meant that he was an idiot.

[A couple of Hermès boxes tumble from a shelf, and after we gather the contents together and replace them she finds a printed-out manuscript in one of them and hands it to me.]

Okay. Here. Here, you can have it. It's in English.

S: What is this?
D: The book I was telling you about, about Tolstoy. Because I wanted to make a movie out of it. Actually, I should publish that. I'm going to give it to someone to publish.

S: So you want to keep it?
D: Yes, I want it back.

[I hand it back.]

S: Do you have a favourite bookshop in Paris?
D: Yes, L'Écume des Pages. It's on Boulevard Saint-Germain. Not La Hune, which is next to it.

S: Could you describe it to me? Why is it the best?
D: I guess it's the editing of it. It's like a magazine. It's always interesting, and I just like the way they show things... Do you know Viktor Frankl?

S: Only by name.

D: About a year ago, I read a book called *The Choice* because my goddaughter gave it to me, and it's about a woman who is now ninety-four. She's a psychiatrist now, but she went to Auschwitz when she was sixteen with her sister, her mother and her father. And she, just like my mother — this is the first time I ever heard of this — was actually picked out of the line that was going to the gas chamber by Mengele, who is the Angel of Death.

S: That's incredible.

D: So of course, by the time I read the book, I connected with her, and then as she was talking, she was talking about her daughter, and I said, 'But actually, the person I am in common with is not you, because I didn't go to Auschwitz. It's your daughter.' Her daughter is exactly my age and she happened to live not too far from me in the country. So I met her, and of course we have so much in common, you know? Then a month ago I was in LA and I called them. They were in La Jolla. They're both psychiatrists, the 94-year-old and her 74-year-old daughter, and I said, 'I'm going to come and visit you and say hello.' I went to visit her in La Jolla, and it was wonderful. It was just wonderful. There's something about survivors that is unique, and it's about embracing life, no matter what. As long as you live, you are not dead.

S: It's astonishing that you happened to live near to one another.

D: You should read that book. It's fantastic. It's called *The Choice* and it's by Dr Edith Eger. And then afterwards, she met this person called Viktor Frankl. I'd never heard of him. He wrote a very, very famous book called *Man's Search for Meaning*. And this is Viktor Frankl's story. He was a psychiatrist in Vienna and he was married, and his wife was pregnant. They got arrested. He, the wife and the parents. And so he took his manuscript and he put it in his pocket, in his coat. Of course, he arrived in Auschwitz, they took the coat, they took the manuscript. The entire time he was in Auschwitz, and I think he was in Auschwitz for three years, he was obsessed by memorising the manuscript, so that he wouldn't forget it. His wife died. Everybody was killed but him. He survived, and he didn't go to Palestine. He didn't go to America. He went back to Vienna, got back into his apartment, sat at the desk, and in nine days he wrote the book and it became a huge success. It was translated into I don't know how many languages.

S: It's like a Stefan Zweig story, somehow.

D: Yes. Yes. It's the same kind of people. And I mean, his thing is all about life, life, life.

S: I will be sure to read it. I'll definitely read Frankl, and *Oblomov*, and a lot more Zweig.

We've drifted well into the evening and Diane is having dinner with a friend. Back in the living room, she gives me yet more books, including two of her own, which she signs, and we talk about Paris neighbourhoods and the intense whirlwind of her life — as it is now, as it has always been. 'The secret is to pay attention,' she says. 'You pay attention to people. You pay attention to details.' She hugs me goodbye, then walks into the bathroom to start getting ready for dinner, shouting goodbye as I let myself out. It's only a minute to the river, and I take a scenic and meandering walk to a Métro station far more distant than is strictly necessary.

SEB EMINA is the editor-in-chief of *The Happy Reader*.
He lives in Belleville, on the border of Paris's nineteenth
and twentieth arrondissements.

A signed copy is always
more valuable, so the
photographer is pleased.

DIANE'S FAVE SOUND FILES

The fashion titan enjoys the intimate rhythm of audiobooks.
Here is a list of her latest acquisitions.

LIFE WITH PICASSO (1964)
Françoise Gilot and Cartoon Lake

Famously short but prodigiously talented, Pablo Picasso was sexually irresistible, running through muses at a frightening rate and painting them with tenderly observed features, savagely rearranged. Françoise Gilot occupied the muse role for a decade but was an artist in her own right; here an often-painted woman gives a self-portrait that is also a portrait of a legend as lover.

THE ARTIST, THE PHILOSOPHER AND THE WARRIOR (2009)
Paul Strathern

Three giants of the Renaissance meet: Leonardo da Vinci, artist, proto-scientist and all-round savant; Niccolò Machiavelli, author of political schemer's bible *The Prince*; and Cesare Borgia, soldier and statesman. The book centres around the journey these emblematic figures took through the Bologna mountains, exploring their intersecting lives and the times they lived in and helped to shape. If we call someone a Renaissance man, we mean that as well as presenting a TV show they've put their name to a children's book. This shows us what the term once meant.

THE HIDDEN LIFE OF TREES (2015)
Peter Wohlleben

Ever wandered through the woods and felt the presence of something secret? This book, by forester Peter Wohlleben, explores the social world of trees. He posits the existence of the 'wood wide web', which trees use to warn of danger and exchange nutrition, although not to troll one another or look at images of more attractive trees. Listen out for them next time you're in woodland; that silence you hear is the sound of living things.

IDENTITY (2018)
Francis Fukuyama

Best known to the lay reader for his now doubtful claims about the end of history, Fukuyama is a more complex and thoughtful figure than media pastiche would imply. In this book he turns his attentions to the rise of identity politics, but while he doesn't ignore the campus battles that excite senior commentators, his conservative reputation is belied by his anger at the new wave of authoritarian populists and his call for a fresh understanding and affirmation of human dignity.

EMPIRE OF PAIN (2021)
Patrick Radden Keefe

The Sackler family are philanthropists, pharmacists and drug dealers that make Pablo Escobar look like small fry. The plague of opiate addiction that swept America in recent decades has been blamed on OxyContin, a highly addictive opioid produced by Purdue Pharma, a Sackler family concern. This book delves into the Sacklers' murky business dealings, the largesse that bought them elite respectability, and the lack of financial consequences they faced for their role in turning thousands of Americans into junkies.

THE CHANCELLOR (2021)
Kati Marton

Angela Merkel could sometimes seem a politician from a different age: consensual, pragmatic, but with a solid core of principles. This biography takes us from her youth in the then GDR to being Chancellor of a united Germany, where she governed in a way that rejected the dogmatism of party allegiance and, perhaps most importantly, provided Europe with moral leadership on the issue of refugees. A politician from a different age then, but whether that age is the past or the future remains to be seen.

BOTH/AND (2021)
Huma Abedin

Huma Abedin is the daughter of Islamic scholars who found herself at the centre of American power. Aide to Hillary Clinton for many years, her memoir gives us the expected tales of White House life and encounters with the great, but also details her marriage to politician and eventual sex offender Anthony Weiner. Not just a glimpse into top-level statecraft, but also a reminder that for every great woman there's a man who can't keep his flies up.

THE WILL TO MEANING (1969)
& YES TO LIFE (1946)
Viktor E. Frankl

Viktor E. Frankl may not be a household name to match Freud's, but he has some claim to be the most significant psychiatric thinker since the sage of the sofa passed away. Frankl's innovation was to make the quest for meaning central to the human mind, an emphasis that coincided with the post-war intellectual world's brief infatuation with existentialism. Unlike some of the more dilettante figures of the café and lecture hall, Frankl's beliefs had been tested in the hellish crucible of the Shoah, in which much of his family died. This gives the commitment to human understanding found in his books the weight of moral heroism; his was a mind that strived for meaning, even when in the power of terror at its most meaningless.

THE LION (1958)
Joseph Kessel

Interspecies understanding is the theme of this novel by Joseph Kessel, now remembered as the creator of *Belle de Jour*. Patricia has a friendship with a lion named King, who she has raised from his days as a cub. Human complications ensure the lion's death and, with it, the death of Patricia's idealised view of the African plains. It is perhaps no coincidence the book came out in 1958, the year the French Union of overseas colonies was dissolved. A process of disillusionment was needed, even at the cost of some innocence.

MEMOIRS OF HADRIAN (1951)
Marguerite Yourcenar

This book is presented as the lost autobiography of the emperor and wall-builder, and it is a tribute to its uncanny ventriloquism that, while we are reading, we forget that the author was a person named Marguerite Yourcenar at all. Until we close the book we are convinced that this is Hadrian, his thoughts, his meditations on the world around him and his great love for Antinous. This is literature as seance, a voice from the dead.

PUTIN V. THE PEOPLE (2019)
Samuel A. Greene and Graeme B. Robertson

The botoxed villain of our nightmares, Vladimir Putin sometimes seems as immovable as his features, his grip on power tight and absolute. This book makes the case that Putin's rule is more fragile than it appears, and does so by looking at the often ignored ordinary Russian. Dealing with protests, shifts in policy and periodic eruptions of violence, it reveals a leader whose road may soon run out.

THE STORY OF MY EXPERIMENTS WITH TRUTH (1948)
Mahatma Gandhi

Often described as Gandhi's autobiography, readers should note that this takes his life up to 1915, missing out the great struggle for Indian independence. What we get instead is Gandhi the thinker and Gandhi the man. We learn much of how he came to the ideals of non-violence and passive resistance that proved so effective, but are also given a picture of a good-hearted, earnest and slightly cranky Edwardian autodidact, visiting vegetarian restaurants in London, reading Ruskin and Tolstoy, and arriving at the eccentric mixture of radicalism and piety that would change the world in ways he would only partly have wished.

THE PLAGUE (1947)
Albert Camus

It was once easy enough to read this book as an allegory; the plague was fascism. Grasp that and we grasp the book. Reading it again in years blighted both by resurgent fascism and a pandemic, you notice how much Camus got right about both. Never has a feeling of unreality been rendered so realistically, never has powerlessness been so powerfully drawn. It is impossible to forget the sickness-haunted streets of Oran; impossible, also, to forget the final warning that the plague can come again.

THE HAPPY
READER

Nella Larsen's novel PASSING is centrifuge to a series of
code-switching stories highlighting the puzzling nature of identity.

AUTHOR

Nella Larsen dedicated *Passing* to two friends, the writer and photographer Carl Va[n]
and his wife, the actress Fania Marinoff. These portraits were captured by the former
moments in 1932. A famous socialite, Van Vechten played a key role in promoting the H[ar]
naissance to white audiences through his oft-controversial writings, and, after switchi[ng]
camera at the age of 51, photographed many of its leading luminaries. His intimate yet
formal treatment of his subjects would often involve bespoke Matisse-inspired backdrop[s]

INTRO

How a novel about race caused a major stir in 1929, only to then be forgotten and for its author to effectively vanish. SEB EMINA introduces Nella Larsen's *Passing*, now recognised as one of the greatest books of the Harlem Renaissance.

BEYOND BINARIES

The international date line is not straight but runs north to south in an inconsistent zigzag. It's on the map, but if you sail west from Hawaii or east from Tonga to look for it that's not going to work: there's nothing actually there. Imaginary lines are powerful.

In Nella Larsen's *Passing*, a pair of friends from childhood run into one another in a hotel bar in Chicago. They lost touch years ago. Both are light-skinned Black women: the scene is a 'white' hotel in the 1920s. Irene exists on the Black side of the colour line. She is married with two children and lives in New York. She organises charity balls and dines with influential people. Aside from discreet transgressions, like glasses of iced tea in white hotels, she moves through the world as a respected member of the Black middle class.

Clare has passed into the white world. Her white husband, a proud racist, has no knowledge of her background. Her reinvention brings material benefits and a strange sort of freedom: she can do anything she likes, except be honest about who she is. Lonely, and desperate to belong, she inveigles herself into Irene's social circle, a development she must keep secret from her husband. It's less a return to her authentic self than a new layer of deception, a doubling-up of double lives.

Passing is fiction but has that feeling some novels have: like it could have happened, like it may as well have happened, so isn't it a true story, then, even if it's not? Nobody knows how many people chose to move from the Black world to the white one. The stories were mostly secret by definition, so novels such as *Passing* and James Weldon Johnson's *The Autobiography of an Ex-Colored Man* stood in.

The subject was uncomfortable, and still is. Larsen was writing at a time when the one-drop rule, which defined a Black person as anyone with even a single Black ancestor, was a fundamental organising principle of American society. When we call Clare and Irene Black, it is by that measure, and while the two friends' ancestry is never completely specified, it's possible, probable even, that Clare and Irene would not be categorised as such today. Larsen describes Clare using phrases like 'the blonde beauty out of the fairy tale', and when people meet Irene outside of Black society, she is taken for 'an Italian, a Spaniard, a Mexican, or a gipsy'. (Reading that list, I, who definitely moves through the world in the Europe of 2022 as a white person, but who had one Nigerian grandparent so would certainly have been on Clare and Irene's side of the colour line if transposed into their situation, thought: I get that too. Am I 'passing' in some way?)

Like Clare, Nella Larsen was brought up by a white family; like Irene, she moved in impressive circles. She grew up with her Danish mother in a working-class Chicago neighbourhood. Of her father, who disappeared when she was two, not much is known, except that he was probably mixed-race and from the Dutch West Indies. To be the biracial child of a white single mother was tough, yet in adulthood Larsen moved to Harlem in New York and became part of a high-flying social and cultural scene. She married a famous physicist, worked as a librarian with the New York Public Library — still a rare career for a Black woman — and was heavily involved in the library's first exhibition of African American artists. The novels she wrote, *Quicksand* and *Passing*, established her as one of the most important writers of the Harlem Renaissance.

Passing is not only a story about race. It is at least as much concerned with what a person might be, independent of the performances they put on for others, and suggests the answer might be: not a hell of a lot. The practice of passing comes in many forms. Is it sexual tension we're picking up between Clare and Irene? Is Irene's relationship with her husband real, or simply an imitation of what they think it ought to be? Last year saw the release of an acclaimed movie adaptation for Netflix directed by Rebecca Hall (a British actress whose maternal grandfather had passed as white) and starring Tessa Thompson as Irene and Ruth Negga as Clare. Many commented how Clare's statements about passing could be applied almost exactly to the transgender experience.

As a working-class, mixed-race woman without a college degree, Larsen did not fit easily into the world of Black intellectuals. Even with two acclaimed novels behind her, she suffered from imposter syndrome. This was only amplified when she found herself in the middle of a plagiarism scandal relating to a short story written not long after *Passing* was published. The case never came to much but despite subsequently becoming the first African American woman to receive a Guggenheim fellowship, Larsen's confidence was shot. She abandoned a third novel, and — by now also divorced — exiled herself from highbrow society. Correspondences from old friends, such as the photographer Carl Van Vechten, went unanswered, and she returned to her original career as a nurse, vanishing (or passing) back into ordinary life.

That life ended when she was seventy-two. She had been lying on the bed in her ground floor apartment in Manhattan. It was 1964. Her work had fallen out of print. The world seemed to have forgotten all about her except for the occasional mention in scholarly studies of Harlem Renaissance literature. She would never see her book rediscovered, reappraised and embraced as a modernist classic. She could never have imagined that, in 2018, the *New York Times* would publish a belated obituary, though perhaps she would not have been surprised when it called her 'a woman whose entire life had been a story of swift erasure'.

DICTION

ADVENTURES IN TELEPHONY

When you speak to someone on the phone, how does your voice paint a picture? Does it change the way that person acts? The way they think? Designer and influencer WILLY NDATIRA on how he abandoned the veneer known as 'white voice'.

1. PLUMBER

When I opened the door to my flat in Johannesburg, the man with his toolbox looked at me with what I would describe was a mix of horror and surprise. 'You sounded like a rich white lady on the phone!' he said. To which I responded, 'You sounded attractive, yet you're not. So, here we are, both disappointed.'

What had happened is that I, a six-foot-two Black guy, had inadvertently used my white voice when I called the plumber. I had tightened my vocal cords, enunciated every word and adopted a higher pitch than usual. The tone was more clipped, more entitled. It was as if I was about to ask to speak to the manager if things didn't go my way.

His comment made me feel like I was in an episode of MTV's *Catfish*, that I was the catfish, he the victim who fell for my subterfuge.

But 'catfishing' is deliberately pretending to be someone you're not in order to develop a relationship with someone else online. Sometimes it is a financial scam; sometimes it is for emotional or psychological reasons.

In my case I had unknowingly codeswitched and made a white South African plumber rush to my flat to fix a leaking washing machine. He rushed because he thought I was a rich white woman. The mistake was his.

But his misapprehension was typical. 'Voices aren't just sounds,' Olivia Kang, a neuroscientist at Harvard who studies hidden biases, has said. 'In a lot of ways, they're auditory faces.' When people hear a voice on the phone, they try to piece together what the other person looks like, how old they are, their gender, where they come from. But you can also form impressions about character: how intelligent someone is, how competent, how likeable, how trustworthy. And in the case of the plumber who rushed to fix my washing machine, you could apparently even tell how rich a person was. His imagination was so vivid he had visualised my bank balance, just by talking to me over the phone.

For obvious reasons these impressions can be flawed. They can even be faked. In the movie *Sorry to Bother You*, Cassius Green, played by LaKeith Stanfield, has landed a job as a telemarketer. At first, he fails to sell any of the encyclopedias he's supposed to peddle. Then a wizened co-worker, Langston, played by Danny Glover, offers him life-changing advice: 'Use your white voice.' White voice is an ideal that not even the white man can attain, Langston says: 'It's what they wish they sounded like, what they're supposed to sound like.' Whiteness is a remote and impossible and crazy-making hope, it's an ideal thrust upon all races. It's privilege, confidence, the

Willy's old apartment

feeling that the world is your oyster and no doors have ever been slammed in your face, at least not based on race.

As for the plumber, the doorway he was standing in led into a five-bedroom apartment with a breathtaking view of Johannesburg on the top floor of a historical building. It was itself proof that not only can the white voice be faked but that it really does open doors.

2. APARTMENT

If I had spoken in my normal voice, the elderly Greek lady who owned the apartment wouldn't have given me a chance to even view it, let alone rent it. I could tell. I saw her surprised look when I arrived, the one that said, 'The voice does not match the race. What do I do?' Yet in the end she rented me the place and that led to an unusual friendship. She moved to a smaller flat down the road, and I would have tea every month with her. When I came over, she would show me her photographs and tell me about her dead husband and her past life in Zambia. She was lonely: her children and grandchildren had moved abroad. I liked her beehive (a wig) and her feistiness. I rented her grand family apartment for four years. I renovated it, redecorated it, and it was even featured in a few magazines. In the end she realised that Blackness is not that different. It's just that it is unsettling to some white people because of their ignorance or closed-mindedness.

What white people often ignore is that Black people, or people of colour in general, are not able to guess who will choose to be racist. From landlords to policemen to employers: to us the world is one lucky or unlucky packet, where instead of a prize we get a racist person or situation to deal with. If it was up to us, it would never happen.

Toni Morrison called it a distraction: 'The function, the very serious function of racism, is distraction. It keeps you from doing your work. It keeps you explaining, over and over again, your reason for being. Somebody says you have no language and you spend twenty years proving that you do. Somebody says your head isn't shaped properly, so you have scientists working on the fact that it is. Somebody says you have no art, so you dredge that up. Somebody says you have no kingdoms, so you dredge that up. None of this is necessary. There will always be one more thing.'

Racism does not always require a face-to-face encounter. When I switched to my white voice during phone calls, I was trying to avoid linguistic profiling. Code-switching is a tool that can help people achieve access to things that were previously closed to them. It may not alter their identity but simply be an additional form of communication that they use when necessary. In my twenties and thirties I used it to get hotel bookings, restaurant reservations and, in this case, the apartment of my dreams. As I saw it, I was applying lessons learned from my parents, who had gone from war refugees to successful business owners in South Africa. They had moved to a seaside town where we were the first Black family to move into a white neighbourhood. The neighbours would empty their trash onto our lawn on a weekly basis in a bid to intimidate us, to make us move elsewhere. We stayed. For years at her local church, my mother was shown a seat at the back. She sat there, on her own, week after week, until one day a white lady plucked up the courage to sit next to her. She kept going to that church until attitudes changed. My siblings and I thought she was a masochist. Why be in a place where you're not wanted? But her lesson was that when faced with racism, stand your ground, occupy your space, and remember that it isn't a reflection on you but the signs of a maladjusted society, or individuals within it.

I don't use my white voice any more. A person might be able to tell my race from listening to my voice, but that doesn't tell them anything about my character. I am not prepared to jump through hoops for racist people. Instead of changing the way people talk, maybe we should change the way people listen. Who says that white voice is best?

3. PARTY

That apartment was my home. It was also my design studio. Since graduating from fashion school, I had been mentored by one of the best couturiers in Johannesburg and subsequently I specialised in custom evening gowns and wedding dresses for a wealthy clientele. High-society women had been part of my daily interactions since leaving design school. Their voice and tone were familiar to me.

In 2012 I started the Instagram account @williamcult. It was one of the first accounts to share only photography, art and fashion references, back when most people were sharing what I referred to then as 'the two Ss: selfies and salads'. Since I was a teen, I had been obsessively compiling photography and art files and I decided to share my archive with the world.

The account gained a large following. From Katy Perry to Hans Ulrich Obrist to designers at luxury houses, my visual references served as inspiration to projects, campaigns and fashion collections. As an experiment I had chosen to run the account anonymously: to never share my face, location, age or race.

Trying to guess the identity of the person behind the account became a game. When I asked people to guess my identity, some thought I was a fat white American guy living in a basement, or an obsessive Asian kid with multiple screens, or a bedridden Russian aristocrat. But nobody could imagine that one of the most talked-about social media accounts belonged to a Black guy on his phone in Africa. By remaining incognito I wanted to test the hidden biases in the art and fashion world. I also wanted to give people the space to project an identity onto me.

I moved to London to complete an MA at Central Saint Martins and soon afterwards I, or rather my Instagram alter ego, was invited to a Marc Jacobs party. The woman at the door said I wasn't William Cult. Nobody knows what he looks like, she said. But he certainly didn't look like me.

Based between Johannesburg, Dubai and London, WILLY NDATIRA is a creative consultant for clients including Gucci, and a consulting editor and writer for *The Happy Reader*'s sibling magazine *Fantastic Man*.

Malcolm x Freestyle (Pharaoh's Dance), 2019–20, Awol Erizku. Digital chromatic print © The Artist. Courtesy Ben Brown Fine Arts

ARRANGEMENTS

In the art of AWOL ERIZKU, symbols of America and of Black identity are arranged according to a principle he describes as 'afro-esotericism'. Born in Ethiopia but raised in the South Bronx, Erizku has electrified audiences with his still lives, photography, installation and film work, upending conventions, both artistic and spiritual, to thrilling effect.

Girl with a Bamboo Earring, 2009

Tell Me The Price, 2017

Left: King of the Jungle, 2017

Overleaf: '632', 2020

MILIEU At the time of the Harlem Renaissance, a man took his wife to court claiming he hadn't realised she was Black. The media circus that followed, writes MORGAN JERKINS, was one of a myriad of ways in which race often descended into a kind of spectacle.

RACIAL IDENTITY AS A JURY TRIAL

In 1923, the Liveright Publishing Corporation took out an ad in *The New York Times* to promote *Cane*, one of the most seminal novels of the Harlem Renaissance, touting it as 'a book about Negroes by a Negro'. The author, Jean Toomer, responded with disdain. Toomer was a fair-skinned man who identified himself as 'Negro' on some official documents and 'white' on others. In fact, in a response letter to the publisher, Toomer wrote, 'My racial composition and my position in the world are realities which I alone may determine.' The stance was extraordinary. He refused to be demarcated into a strict racial binary by white gatekeepers.

This act of dissent was part of a shift in racial consciousness — and questioning — that occurred during the Harlem Renaissance, one that had those like Toomer constantly attempting to evade 'rules' and labels.

In the 1920s, Black art was changing at an unprecedented pace, supported by a publishing ecosystem encompassing journals and anthologies such as *The Crisis*, *The New Negro* and *Opportunity*. In 1927, Charles S. Johnson, the editor of the latter, spearheaded a new project called *Ebony and Topaz*. In the magazine, Black writers, thinkers and artists, such as Jessie Fauset and Arna Bontemps, whose work incorporated poetry and fiction, as well as white people of similar vocations, like the dramatist Paul Green and the novelist Julia Peterkin, explored 'the materials of Negro life' through essays, poems and illustrations. In Johnson's introduction to the project, he takes a swipe at two of his peers, Alain Locke and W.E.B. Du Bois, tastemakers with monumental influence over African American artistic production. Both promoted an aspirational Black identity imbued with pride, self-esteem and independence. Although this agenda may seem harmless upon first glance, these men were necessitating a need for one, definite Black character, from which there was very little wiggle room to be much else. In *Ebony and Topaz*, there were no constraints on what the contributors could discuss about Black American life, the idea being to disprove the notion that only one such model existed. Some of the topics explored that Johnson's peers would have considered taboo were homosexuality, Harlem dance halls and mixed-race identity. Some of the most striking illustrations from *Ebony and Topaz* are found in the series *Drawings for Mulattoes* by the gay writer and painter Richard Bruce Nugent. The Black and white subjects — and even the different landscapes in which they inhabit — are mirror images of each other. They are styled in a yin-and-yang aesthetic. The racial hybridity of this illustration, as well as the rest of the collection, suggests that race is not some fixed, calcified state of being. In fact, race as a concept has to be a lie, as it is subject to interpretation that is too varied to be resolutely defined.

In the twenty-first century, we know this to be true: race is a social construct that is not 'real' yet certainly has real consequences. However, the Harlem Renaissance took place at a time when obsession over racial purity and Negro blood had reached an all-time high in American culture. For context, the 1850 census was the first time that the term *mulatto* was used to refer to people of mixed white and Black ancestry. Josiah Nott, a slave owner and 'racial' scientist from Alabama, suspected that white people and Black people were from different species altogether, and wanted to see if mixed-race enslaved people had a different lifespan as a result. He was able to influence Joseph Underwood, a senator from Kentucky, to use the term when counting individuals across the country. Forty years later, in 1890, new categories appeared: *quadroon*, denoting a quarter African ancestry, and *octoroon*, denoting an eighth African ancestry.

It must be stated that these mathematical breakdowns were not uncommon in the Americas. In fact, in the French colony of Saint-Domingue, there were the aforementioned categories as well as *mamelouk* (1/16th), *quarteronné* (1/32nd), *sang-mêlé* (1/64th), *griffe* (3/4th), *marabou* (5/8th) and *sacatra* (7/8th). And then in 1920, in the fourteenth census, the one-drop rule was introduced, meaning that if anyone had any Black ancestry, they were Black. Only 'pure-blooded' whites were considered white. Coincidentally, when the Harlem Renaissance reached its peak in 1924, the Virginia state legislature passed the Preservation for Racial Integrity Act, which stated that a white person is someone who has 'no trace whatsoever of any blood other than Caucasian'. And then by 1930, coincidentally when the Harlem Renaissance was just on the brink of decline, all the racial categories fell away and only 'Negro' remained after white statisticians argued that the other categories were subjective.

The curious case of Kip and Alice Rhinelander tested the limits of the one-drop rule, at least as it related to love and sex. The Rhinelanders were one of the oldest and wealthiest families in New York City, so the expectations were that Leonard, the family's youngest son, would have as his eventual bride someone of a similar status. Yet in 1921, while the bespectacled, awkward man, who most referred to by his nickname Kip, was in Stamford, Connecticut, to work on his stuttering at an inpatient clinic, he met a fair-skinned, dark-haired, working-class maid named Alice with whom he fell in love. Over the course of three years, Kip and Alice kept their relationship alive through secret letters and trysts, until in 1924 they eloped to a city hall in New Rochelle. Their marriage certificate listed them both as white.

Weeks later, reporters began digging into Alice's background and discerned her father was in fact 'coloured'.

Philip Rhinelander, Kip's father, filed a suit claiming Alice had deceived his son into believing that she was white as a way to access the family's wealth. In New York, interracial marriage was not illegal. However, if one individual could claim that their spouse had bamboozled them on a substantive matter prior to marriage, in this instance by pretending to be white, they might have a case. At first, Alice denied the claim and went so far as enlisting the help of her father to delegitimise the naturalisation papers that listed him as coloured. A year later, with the trial underway, Alice changed her defence to counter-argue that Kip always knew about her being 'coloured' because of premarital sex. *The New York Times* printed excerpts from their love letters and stated that in court, 'Rhinelander sat on the stand expressionless, his eyes shielded by his glasses so that no one could see what his thoughts were as he listened to the recital of his one adventure...'

Drawings for Mulattoes — Number 4 (1928)

Although this case has been studied in law schools and was the basis for several films, including 1959's *Night of the Quarter Moon*, the story is relatively overlooked and has been neglected in mainstream circles of the modern era. But the case's implications are eerily prescient. Race is elusive, and no matter how intimate one's relationship is with another person, their identity is malleable. Kip thought that Alice was white due to her appearance. Apparently so did his father, whose main reservation, before finding out about her mixed-race parentage, had been that Alice was of a lower-class status. Indeed, Kip's defence was that he had been tricked, the implication being that Alice acted like any other white woman. And perhaps when they married, for those weeks when he claimed not to know her true ancestry, she carried herself as an upper-class white woman to and from Manhattan and New Rochelle, the city upstate where the Rhinelanders were from, without her new cohorts suspecting anything.

The Civil War may have ended slavery, at least in its American form, but the Reconstruction era that followed it was a period of great terror, as efforts to empower Black Americans to take part in civil society were met with the rise of the Ku Klux Klan, the Knights of the White Camellia, and other white domestic terrorist groups who sought to violate, torture and lynch anyone who dared to threaten the racial hegemony of the antebellum days. For millions of African Americans in the south, this danger propelled them to start migrating to other parts of the country — The Great Migration — and New York City was one of the most attractive spots in which to land. For

The Cotton Club

light-skinned Blacks especially, the opportunity to pass had arisen because the movement away from ancestral homelands in the south allowed them to take on new personas. The Harlem Renaissance provided a lane for more conversation about racial identities and its ambiguities.

Though New York City was not a segregated place like the Jim Crow South, racial mixing was looked down upon by white New Yorkers. However, during the Harlem Renaissance, such commingling took the form of a kind of spectacle. The famous Cotton Club, where, on any given night, Black singers such as Louis Armstrong, Cab Calloway or Bessie Smith would perform, catered to a predominately white audience. In fact, Black men were commonly rejected from being a part of the Cotton Club clientele. One writer of the WPA slave narratives, a Roosevelt-led initiative that funded the collection of ordinary stories during the Depression years, described the scene: 'Mixed parties were OK if the men were WHITE and the women BLACK. When a party was one of WHITE women and BLACK men or even if a Negro man or men were in a party of white men and women, they invoked their charter membership and demanded your card.'

At her notorious Dark Tower parties, A'Lelia Walker, daughter of the entrepreneur Madam C. J. Walker, would serve the white people, who travelled uptown for the festivities, chitlins, pig feet and gin. A clear-cut reason as to why A'Lelia did this has never been discovered. But one could deduce that if privileged white people were travelling uptown to be among Black folks, being served soul food was also a part of the show.

Many of the bars and nightclubs of that time — Taafe's on 113rd and 5th, Barron Wilkins Club on 134th and 7th, and the Astoria Club — catered to the desires of many upper- and middle-class whites to consume what they thought to be authentic Black life. In fact, at the Astoria Club, management arranged the seating so that Black patrons sat in the centre and white people sat in the back; this way, the whites could watch the Black patrons as well as the show.

Even in the literary realm, white voyeurism did not lose its grip. White patrons, such as Charlotte Osgood Mason, sponsored the work of Zora Neale Hurston and Langston Hughes, and had firm expectations of the type of output that she wanted to see. Carl Van Vechten, a writer and photographer most known for his portraits of the Black luminaries of that period, published a novel called *Nigger Heaven* which was supposed to chronicle Black life in Harlem. It sent Black Harlem into an uproar for Van Vechten's portrayals of sex and crime, whereas white critics of the time held the work in good esteem. Regardless of how the book was received, Van Vechten was an example of the way in which well-to-do whites could ingratiate themselves into Black circles for exploitative purposes.

The fetishisation of Black society and the racial hybridity of that era is quite blatant in Nella Larsen's *Passing*. 'You don't know, you can't realise how I want to see Negros, to be with them again, to talk with them, to hear them laugh,' gushes Clare to Irene, while begging for the chance to attend a Harlem social function. Clare, a light-skinned Black woman who passes for white, wants nothing else but for Black people to perform for her. Their presence is entertainment. She wants to consume them.

'What if Bellew should divorce Clare? There was the Rhinelander case,' Irene wonders in another scene, Bellew being a proud racist unaware of his wife's heritage. One might assume that Larsen mentioned *Rhinelander v. Rhinelander* because of its relevance to passing; however, the author's own personal life may have had influence. Like Alice Rhinelander, Larsen, who was born Nellie Larsen in 1891, was of West Indian descent through the patrilineal line. Larsen's mother was Danish. It is not clear if Larsen's parents ever married, but Larsen's father disappeared — or died — when she was still a toddler. When her mother remarried another Dane, Larsen took his last name, but the blending of families did nothing to mediate her in-betweenness as a biracial woman in the world.

In any case, in order to succeed in racial passing, one has to be hypersensitive to others' gazes. And with the story of Alice Rhinelander, judging by how she flip-flopped between arguing that she was in fact white and accusing her former husband of knowing about her Blackness all along, one can see just how tricky and suffocating others' gazes can be, whether on the streets of New York or under the scrutiny of the courtroom.

The *Rhinelander v. Rhinelander* trial came to a head when Alice exposed her nude body from the waist up to the judge and jury as a way of demonstrating that a man who had seen her nipples must surely have been aware of her blackness. The jury agreed, ruling in Alice's favour, and the young couple never saw each other again. Because Kip had not performed in a way that was expected of a white, wealthy man by marrying a coloured woman, he was removed from the *New York Social Register* and banned from a host of exclusive clubs throughout the city. He never remarried or had children, and died at the age of thirty-two from a form of pneumonia. Alice, however, lived until she was seventy-four and received $300 a month in alimony payments. Her death certificate recorded her name as Alice Jones, but her tombstone, in the Beechwoods Cemetery in New Rochelle, still carries the name 'Alice J. Rhinelander', signifying the identity-shifting that characterised her life up to the very end.

MORGAN JERKINS is a *New York Times* bestselling author and former resident of Harlem. Her third and most recent book, *Caul Baby*, a novel, was released in 2021.

FROM NOVEL TO SKETCHBOOK TO MOVIE

Shot poignantly in black and white and released through Netflix, last year's movie adaptation of *Passing* was the directorial debut of English actress Rebecca Hall. It was also the realisation of a long-interrupted ambition. Hall, 40, had originally read *Passing* in her early twenties, at which time she was so shaken by its relevance to her own background (her mother, opera singer Maria Ewing, was mixed-race but often taken to be white) that she immediately sat down and wrote the screenplay. Here, *The Happy Reader* shares exclusive sketches from Hall's own storyboard. Alongside the corresponding stills, shooting notes, and lines from the novel, they offer a raw glimpse into the alchemy that transmutes static prose to moving picture.

TOYSHOP Larsen: 'It was on that day of all others that Irene set out to shop for the things which she had promised to take home from Chicago to her two small sons.'
Hall: 'Close on Irene. Still partially shaded by hat. Pull out to reveal standing in a line.'

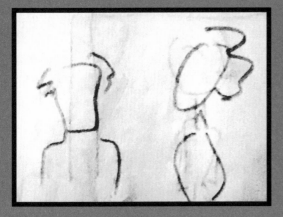 

HOTEL ROOM Larsen: 'My goodness, Jack! What difference would it make if, after all these years, you were to find out if I was one or two per cent coloured?'
Hall: 'Clare and John sitting close. "What difference would it make?" Profile John. Clare in background focussed. Pull out to John to focus for cigarette lighting.'

FLOWERS   Larsen: 'You know you don't mean that, Clare. You're only trying to tease me. I know very well
that I take being a mother very seriously.'
Hall: 'Slow track. "I know I take being a mother..."'

HOTEL BAR   Larsen: 'An attractive looking woman, was Irene's opinion, with those dark, almost black, eyes
and that wide mouth like a scarlet flower against the ivory of her skin.'
Hall: 'Wider on Clare. Close up. Clare keeps staring, makes to stand up.'

STREET   Larsen: 'Brian wrapped his coat around her. She began to cry rockingly, her entire body
heaving with convulsive sobs.'
Hall: 'Brian wraps Irene in a coat. Two shot. All fairly high angle.'

COMPUTING

When big data conjures up identities to manipulate us, the results are monstrous for being actually quite convincing. The proliferation of deepfake people has advanced far more than most of us think, writes technology and culture writer ROISIN KIBERD.

ARTIFICIALNESS

Two pictures appear on the screen, on the website whichfaceisreal.com. On the left is a girl with pale pink skin, sandy hair and tortoiseshell glasses. On the right is a man with a dark beard, uneven teeth, and eyes the colour of ink.

Which picture is real, and which is of someone who has never existed? I'm leaning towards choosing the girl as the imposter; the skin around her chin is oddly creased, like that of someone many decades older. It's only when I zoom in that I realise I'm wrong. Up close, the man's face is covered in lines like stretch marks. There's a blue, bruise-like shadow along his nose. His teeth are not just uneven; they're warped, with a narrow half-tooth suspended between two incisors. I feel suddenly disturbed by the sight of him. The man is a replicant, a fake, a product of a synthetic reality.

In my dreams, the people rarely have faces. On this website, the dream of a machine, a new face is generated every two seconds. They're created by software called StyleGAN. Trained on a dataset of 70,000 photos, it consists of two neural networks, collections of algorithms made to mimic the human brain.

With time it gets easier to differentiate the humans and imposters; the automated faces have asymmetries, pronounced skin texture, backgrounds that are blurred or indistinct. In one portrait of a middle-aged man his right earlobe is twice the size of his left one. In another, a dark object hovers above a woman's head, shapeless, unidentifiable. Each element of human identity is there – age, gender, race – but they're touched by machine-logic, details taken out of context by an inhuman mind.

Already, the StyleGAN faces are being used by marketers as stock imagery, and by cybercriminals as the faces of fake social media accounts. In 2019, Facebook removed a network of thousands of accounts for 'inauthentic behaviour' – many of them had StyleGAN profile pictures. Even LinkedIn, perhaps the most drab, uneventful place on the internet, has been infiltrated by spies with AI-generated faces; an AP report from 2019 identified a Washington-based 'policy expert' named Katie Jones, who didn't exist but who had successfully befriended a number of high-ranking US state officials.

Sometimes I look into these faces and perceive them as warnings, auguries of a future when everything will be unreal. We're almost ready; we look for Photoshop in Instagram pictures; we distrust news stories and marketing claims; we enjoy unnatural flavours; we laugh at the sentimental contents of our spam folders, the lonely men, women and robots who promise us the world.

Then again, this isn't a future. It's a present; one where human traits are manufactured on a superhuman scale. Where the benign words of customer service chatbots and friendly ASMR videos offer comfort, each day, as we work in competition with machines. Where technology has harnessed our empathy, our anger, and has turned them into data, and where we tell our secrets to systems with a human face.

ROISIN KIBERD's first book, *The Disconnect*, was published by Serpent's Tail in 2021. She grew up in Dublin and lives in Berlin, and is currently learning to raise carnivorous plants.

TRAVEL The grey gates of departures, the crude assumptions of strangers: a story by GABRIELLE BELLOT shows that travelling is also, often, an act of passing.

THROUGH SECURITY

A few days later, when a female TSA agent's hands are cradling my crotch outside an airport body scanner in Togo on my way back to the United States because my transgender body has been flagged as an 'anomaly', I briefly remember the grinning man in Île de Gorée.

A small island off the coast of Senegal famed — and infamous — for its colonial-era exhibitions, Gorée is where my partner and I have decided to visit for a day trip outside of Dakar, the chaotic city my partner's sister lives in. We are visiting Senegal for a week, and Gorée seems like it will have a special connection with me, a multiracial girl from a Caribbean island formerly colonised by both the British and the French. It is my first time in Africa, and I've yearned to see a bit of the world that — through the horrors of the slave trade — has so shaped my own.

From the start, the trip to Senegal is complicated. As a trans woman in a relationship with a white cis woman travelling to a country where it is not safe to be openly queer, I must pass both as a woman and as straight to avoid danger; I also do not know if people will see

Île de Gorée

my melange of features as Black, white, Latina or something else entirely. A few minutes after we get off the ferry to Gorée, a man appears out of a shadowy hall and launches, unprompted, into a baroque exegesis on the transatlantic slave trade, pointing out a building and explaining that it was where Africans were held before being shipped off to the Americas. We politely thank him for his information and try to walk away, but he follows, grinning and pointing out other areas and beckoning us to follow him into sombre-looking buildings.

Ironically, as I learn later, Gorée, for all of its museum-like pomp, probably didn't play a significant role in the history of the transatlantic slave trade, but because this belief serves local tourism well, the Senegalese government has encouraged the narrative that Gorée was an indispensable piece of history. The island, in a way, is also passing.

Despite this, after a few more minutes of his extemporaneous tour, he asks us with a smile to pay him for his efforts. After my partner repeats for the tenth time that we didn't request a tour, his face hardens like a gargoyle's, and he says he hates her and calls her a white devil. Before I can react to this remarkable volte-face, he turns to me, unceremoniously grinning again. 'Sister,' he says, 'surely you understand…'

I am visibly mixed, my light brown skin and hanging corkscrew curls a canvas upon which one can write almost any ethnicity with a question mark, and in this moment I have passed not simply as a woman but as Black. Of course, I reflect later, passing here is a kind of capitalistic convenience: the man clearly wished to appeal to my racial sympathies, his 'sister' a bridge towards him receiving compensation. He only leaves after many more attempts to get away, branding my partner a white demon one final time.

I am left unsure, in this bewildering moment of guilt, sadness and fury at his insults, what to make of it all, except I know that the ghost of passing feels like it is hovering near me, cold and strange under the West African sun.

Days later, in the airport trying to get to our connecting flight in Togo, I am gripped by that phantasmal chill again. As a trans woman, airport body-scanning machines unnerve me: the agents select a gender for you before scanning you based on sight, and your body is expected to conform to certain expectations for cisgender people, like having a vagina if you are labelled a 'woman' or having straight hair rather than an afro, and if it does not, your offending area may be labelled an 'anomaly', prompting your strange body to be patted down. To lessen the likelihood of this labelling, I try to wear tighter underwear than normal and to 'tuck' what is down there; done right, I won't be flagged by the machines, but it's always a toss-up.

As the TSA agent pats around my thighs, then almost cups my genital region in her hands, she pauses, then removes her fingers. 'Oh, it's a man,' she says aloud. In my fear and fury, I do not wait to hear more; I grab my stuff from the security bin and almost run to the plane, not even bothering to put my slippers back on.

I am lucky, I realise, because it does not seem as if the other TSA agents heard the woman. Had they, I might have been questioned, even detained for examination,

because this, like the island I grew up on, is a place where bodies like mine are not supposed to exist, where we are assumed to be deceiving others by how we dress, and passing is no mere convenience, but a survival mechanism.

As I sit on the plane, trying not to cry, I think about how I succeeded in passing in one place and failed in the other, but then I do not really know if I have succeeded at all, have passed the test of passing, because in a better world I would not need to worry about passing as anything at all. But in this one, that ghost, instead, is always near me, reminding me that I will always confound and confuse people, and all I can hope is that I never confound the person who will respond with fists rather than with questions.

GABRIELLE BELLOT is a staff writer for *Literary Hub* and a contributing editor at *Catapult*. She first read *Passing* a few years into transitioning.

Canadian writer WAYDE COMPTON on how the word 'passing' shapes reality, smuggling unfair preconceptions into the way we talk about race.

A BETTER WORD

English has just one word to describe the way in which a person of one race can be seen as being of a different race: from the United States, we get the word *passing* — as in, 'He has Black ancestry but he can pass for white.' You can hear in the term echoes of the repressive history that created it. Yet *passing* is used pervasively and expansively because there is no other word that specifically applies to this phenomenon.

But it is a troubling term: *passing* forces a syntax in which the *person looking* is erased while the *person seen* is made the subject. Because if I am standing in line at the bank and you decide I am white when I am actually half-Black, this language forces me to say that in this situation, *I passed for white*. It eliminates

your act of looking. In fact, it erases *you* entirely from the wording. But this is absurd. If a viewer is deciding what race they think a person looks like, then the viewer should own the verb.

This is why I coined the verb *pheneticize* — borrowing from a biological classification method — to replace *passing* in such situations. If you see me in line at the bank and decide I am white when I am actually half-Black, then you are *pheneticizing* me as white. It is something *you* are doing.

We can and should reserve the word *passing* for cases when a racially ambiguous person actively chooses to lie about their identity. In that sense, the word *passing* still has a use. But in situations where it is the viewer who is

TO CATCH THE GAZE

The first edition of *Passing*, published in 1929 by Alfred A. Knopf, has a cover consisting of simply a decorative pattern and a few words of text. It was an understated design at a time when Harlem Renaissance novels usually had jackets that signalled their status as such. Larsen's book received rave reviews before being largely forgotten, resurfacing at the end of the 1960s thanks only to a copyright technicality. New editions followed with accelerating frequency, their jackets synthesising modern audiences' perceived interests with new fashions in book design. Sometimes these suggested a book somewhat different to the one actually being printed, as with the Collier cover promising a 'searing novel of racial conflict in the 1930s'. As the novel gained canonical standing, translations appeared in languages such as French, Hebrew and Japanese, adding yet more modes to the ways the book met the eyes of readers. Recent ebook covers appear to have been designed by artificial intelligence, perhaps according to algorithmic concerns, with baffling results. Still, a book is not its cover, a fact somewhat entwined with the messages and meanings we might take away when we pick up *Passing* and actually read it.

Alfred A. Knopf, 1929

Penguin Classics, 2018

Macmillan Collector's
Library, 2020

Modern Library, 2002

Sellerio editore Palermo,
1995

Meirovich, 2014

Athar Classics, 2016

Penguin Vitae, 2020

Signet, 2021

Irmás Cartoné, 2017

Collier Books, African / American Library, 1971

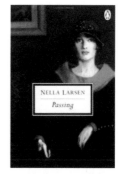

Penguin Twentieth-Century Classics, 1997

Imã Editorial, 2020

Nieuw Amsterdam, 2018

WLC, African American Heritage Classics, 2010

Misuzu Shobo, 2022

Am Oved, 2017

Digital Fire, 2021

Harper Collins Português, 2020

Sperling & Kupfer, 2020

Sublime Books, 2013

Dörlemann, 2021

Vintage Classics, 2022

Reading Essentials, 2018

assuming things about those they examine, then that viewer should own the action.

Furthermore, even in situations that might aptly be described as passing — where the subject does indeed choose to identify themselves as a race they are not — the real story is often far more complex than the word suggests, and involves acts of identification from without. And often, when we look closely, such stories begin with how an individual is pheneticized, long before they choose to actively pass themselves — and the pheneticization itself is a motivating factor in their ostensibly clear case of passing.

One example I use is the case of Marie Joseph, a Qayqayt woman who, while living in Vancouver's Chinatown in the mid-20th century, eventually chose to pass for Chinese. This Indigenous women married a Chinese man and took on that racial identity herself in the wake of the traumatic experience of her nation being delisted by the Canadian government. While she did indeed come to project herself as Chinese, the first inkling that this might be possible for her was because people assumed she was Chinese when she was working in a restaurant as a waitress in Chinatown. This planted a seed, and offered a way out of the particular kind of oppression she faced at

that time, and she made the shift. But how she was initially pheneticized by others played an inciting role in her decision.

Another case is that of Chief Buffalo Child Long Lance (Sylvester Long), often described as a Black man who passed for Indigenous in the early twentieth century. While he did come to lie about which Indigenous nation he belonged to, along with many other aspects of his life story, the truth is that he did have Indigenous ancestry mixed with Black. It was American society that designated his family as Black, due to its own racial binaries often based on appearance over ancestry. It can be argued that he was pheneticized by American society as Black, yet chose to identify as Indigenous. In his case, the story is simplistically rendered if you remove how he was viewed and racially overdetermined — that is, how he was pheneticized — from the experiences that motivated his life choices, in what is ostensibly a standard passing narrative.

Award-winning writer WAYDE COMPTON is the author of five books and the editor of two literary anthologies. He first coined the term 'pheneticizing' in 2010 in the book *After Canaan: Essays on Race, Writing, and Region*.

FAMILY

The lie that GEORGINA LAWTON was told by her parents burrowed so deep into her sense of herself it worked as a kind of disguise in reverse. She believed it, but others didn't.

BELIEVING MY EYES

Long before I became acquainted with Nella Larsen's book *Passing*, I was passing myself. Passing is usually associated with a very particular era in American racial history, but in my case it occurred in a leafy section of suburban Surrey on the borders of south London, and formed the backdrop to my upbringing. I grew up in a very white, very British household with married parents and a younger brother. My mother is from the west coast of Ireland. My father had grown up in Shropshire and Somerset. I was raised

within the soft womb of whiteness along with my blue-eyed brother: a cul-de-sac childhood with Sunday roasts, bike lessons with my father and an education at a Catholic girl's secondary school in Carshalton where I had many friends. We took summer holidays to Ireland and Spain and ate dinner as a family. On the exterior things looked idyllic and in many ways they were — except for the fact I was passing for white.

I first remember discussing the colour of my skin with another child in my primary school playground when she advised me to 'scratch myself white'. It's a scene I can still recall vividly, even though it was almost twenty-five years ago. It also serves to remind me of the psychological hold parents have over their children. We believe what we are told to believe. At age five, I was barely cognisant of the concept of race, but when my parents told me I 'wasn't Black' I believed them. I understood that I was different, I could see I was the only child at school who looked like me, but I believed my parents when they told me I was like them. I wanted to belong. And so I believed that 'whiteness' was not just a skin colour, but a category into which I was accepted — at least at home. A child's identity is fragile, their worlds limited to just home and school. In my early years I knew that I wanted to belong with the family who claimed me, and so I returned to my class the next day and defensively repeated my heritage to my classmates: I was white because my family was, and they had claimed me — and that was that. I learned to wear my story like armour when challenged by others. As I grew older, many of the same friends from primary school joined me at secondary school, dutifully adopting the family lore I had been encouraged to swallow at home. I was fully embedded in whiteness and seemed to pass as white in my community, but outside the home I began to notice that I could not pass as white because it did not make sense. I was the only brown face in family photos in Ireland and the UK, at my church group, at childhood birthday parties and at my keyboard lessons. I quickly learned that I could not escape race, and in fact, with each year, race became increasingly dogged in its pursuit of me. Often this took the form of isolating moments of reckoning in which I would be marked out as an outsider: beside my brother in an airport aged ten when a security worker ushered me towards the Black family in front of mine; the moment when time stood still as I was called a racial slur in Ireland; all the times I was asked, 'What's your mix?' or 'Are you adopted?' But my parents could not acknowledge what was happening to me: any mention of race or racism caused my mother to walk out of the room and my father to affirm his love for me while shutting down any further discussion. For years I walked a thin racial tightrope, being identified as a minority beyond the home, while somehow also passing as a white member of a white family, and the daughter of both my parents within it.

This might not make sense to many because I am not white-passing. In the traditional sense, racial passing necessitates that you look like the group you are attempting to pass into. But in an essay called 'Race-ing and Being Raced: The Critical Interrogation of Passing', Teresa Kay Williams, Professor of Sociology and Ethnic Studies at UCLA, supports stories like mine. She notes that passing occurs beyond 'phenotypical ambiguity', and can exist in various forms. 'Passing can occur based on physical appearance,

Carshalton, Surrey

cultural display, or both. The participants, their intentions and motivations and the social context within which passing occurs must all be interactively understood because "passing" does not necessitate taking place objectively, consistently, or even rationally,' she writes. To anyone who could see me, it was apparent that I was not white, so logically I should not have passed, but passing is not entirely logical. It can relate to the cultural and is dependent largely on acceptance from the group into which someone is attempting to gain access to. I was not trying to pass — my parents made the decision for me — but they were the adults, and they set the tone for the adults around them, too. No one in Ireland or the UK — grandparents, cousins, aunties or uncles — really challenged my place in the family, because they took their cues from my parents, who had adopted a policy of racial silence when I was born.

When I reached my early teens I became more cynical. A raceless existence had been de rigueur in the home, but beyond it I was starting to become radicalised. I studied politics and learned that whiteness as a concept and a system of power would never, and had never, accepted those who looked like me and

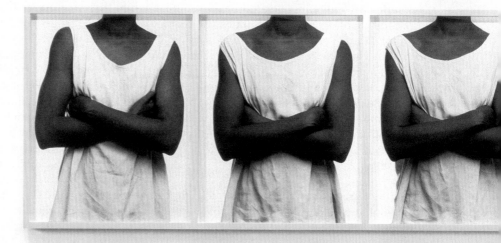

MISDESCRIPTION   MISINFORMATION   MISIDENTIFY   MISDIAGNOSE   MISFUNCTION   MISTRA

THURSDAY

FRIDAY

MISREMEMBER   MISGAUGE   MISCONSTRUE   MISTRANSLATE

FIVE DAY FORECAST

The elusive nature of identity and the subtle power of anonymity are among motifs at play in Lorna Simpson's artwork *Five Day Forecast*. Originally displayed in 1991, it belongs to an oeuvre often exploring a similar thematic universe to *Passing*, by one of the first Black female artists to reach the top tier of the American art world.

Five Day Forecast, 1988
© Lorna Simpson. Courtesy the artist and Hauser & Wirth.

nor should I want it to. My mother switched her story when I pressed for more details around the mystery of my birth. 'You might be a genetic throwback,' she said. 'Your dark skin could have come from a distant ancestor in Ireland.' This Irish-throwback story embedded me further into my Irish heritage and prevented me from pushing for answers, but it did not justify my dark skin and afro-curly hair, nor did it prevent me from detesting my appearance. I tried to diet my way out of my fuller figure and wider hips and bleach the curls out of my hair. Whiteness was aspirational; its hold over my life was omnipresent.

When I reached university I still didn't know. Then, in my second year, my father was diagnosed with incurable cancer. I felt I could no longer uphold a nebulous family narrative. His illness became the catalyst for uncovering the truth and a series of distressing DNA tests after his death in 2016 proved what many naysayers had long claimed: my mum had been concealing an affair with a Black man she had once known. I had been robbed of both my identity and my biological ties to my father and his family, and also of my life story. I had been passing as white in both the physical and cultural sense as a child and as my father's daughter. Unlearning everything I had been told was like learning to walk again in my early twenties. Everything was off-balance.

In the America of the eighteenth and nineteenth centuries, racial passing was often a vital act for safety and protection. For many, it meant disappearing without a trace: estimates on the number of Blacks who passed in the USA vary wildly. At the heart of all the stories there is deception, but there is also immeasurable loss. As the scholar Allyson Hobbs argues in *A Chosen Exile: A History of Racial Passing in American Life*, passing is not becoming what you pass for, but losing what you passed from. My route to whiteness as designed by my parents conferred social entitlements — I had anglicized names, parents who looked like all my teachers at school, an ease with which I could navigate many white circles — but it also came at the expense of loss of community, culture and self. I was ashamed of my skin and stayed away from other people of colour who tried to claim me for many years because they could see that I was not able to pass in

the way my parents wished. Being passed off, as I was, requires a 'passer' (a parent) to make the choice for the 'passee' (the child). The passee is denied agency, but being passed off also requires participation from a range of others to uphold a story which warps worlds. Upon learning that my father was not my own, I felt as if all my interactions with my wider family had been disfigured, that I was uncovering a conspiracy in which everyone had been assigned a key role. Being passed off is destabilising and it requires everyone to sustain fragile and false realities. When I realised I couldn't pass as white, I came to the depressing conclusion that it meant I couldn't pass as the son or daughter of my white parents. Accepting that at first was too painful. It would have meant deconstructing not only my personal identity but the world into which I passed. That is why it took me a lifetime to unravel the truth on my own.

Years later, when I began researching the stories of Black and brown kids like me, who had been passed off as something they were not by parents and caregivers, I was taken to the bookshop Foyles by the publisher Sharmaine Lovegrove. I was struggling to find my writing voice and embarrassed by what I thought was a uniquely depressing personal lore. Sharmaine bought me a copy of Nella Larsen's *Passing* to encourage me to write, but also, I think, to help me feel a little less alone. I recall her saying, 'Your story is the story of so many others.'

That first time I read Larsen's story of Black women who were able to pass in the America of the 1920s, I realised there are many parallels between those lives and my own. In piecing together my identity and repairing my relationship with my family, however, there's one paragraph I always come back to: 'Pain, fear, and grief were things that left their mark on people. Even love, that exquisite torturing emotion, left its subtle traces on the countenance.'

GEORGINA LAWTON is the author of the memoir *Raceless* as well as *Black Girls Take World*, a travel manual for Black women. She is a regular *Guardian Weekend* contributor, and hosts the popular podcast *The Secrets In Us.*

LETTERS

Messages received from Brooklyn and Saint Petersburg.

Dear *Happy Reader*

I wrote my undergraduate thesis on *Middlemarch* (*THR17*). This was at a small Catholic college founded by nuns in Rhode Island, in the Northeastern region of America. We were required to post our thesis presentations on YouTube in the era when YouTube was viewed as a private platform to submit assignments. The video is one of the more humiliating products of my life (one commenter remarks: "She was so nervous .. exactly like me …"), and one of the more resilient — it has over seven years been viewed about 13,500 times. I say this not as proof of my expertise on the topic (I do not claim such), but as an exhibit of evidence that there has long been, and remains, a hungry crowd of web surfers eager to hear about *Middlemarch* from any source.

Middlemarch is, essentially, a book of aphorisms overlaid onto an addictive soap opera. Momentum is sustained by Eliot's kernels of philosophy popping throughout the plot. It couldn't be what it is if you separated one from the other, but I think it is the aphoristic quality that sets it apart from the straightforward readability of Charles Dickens and makes it "for grown-up people" (Woolf, famously). The epigrams alone are their own kind of storyline.

An aphorism is not a full thought system, and its success is measured by how quickly its wit can be apprehended by a reader. This novel is the opposite, its reward building over a 900-page slow burn. The aphorisms are quick hits of philosophy and insight, but the plot is where Eliot's fuller ideas percolate — misspent potential, value of unrecognised accomplishments, the many ways of failing in love. I've always thought this tension to be quite like life, as insights are meted out to us during our march through time.

I long ago lost the login information to that account with my thesis presentation. I sometimes check in on how the video is doing and listen (for as long as I can stand) to the person, now seven years younger than me, who has lots of ideas about *Middlemarch*. A real Dorothea. I'm no longer nearly as idealistic, but still try to remember how much worth she saw in being a foundress of nothing.

Lauren Kane — Brooklyn, New York

Dear Happy Reader,

I'm still keeping my issue 17 unpacked, but feeling very happy about having an opportunity to get it after the beginning of the war. While deferring the moment of joy (could it ever be possible after all of this pain, shame and fear?) I am rereading the story of Ali's *Madonna in a Fur Coat* in the previous issue. The paragraph that parallels the cohort of Ernest Hemingway and the people who went through the virus and lockdown for after-the-end-of-February me is speaking of the newest Lost Generation with postwar trauma. What kind of trauma would it be? What kind of pain does it consist of? Unspeakable and sharp pain of people who've lost their homes and close ones. Dull pain of those who are trapped on the other side: disorientated by the feeling of collective responsibility, being called betrayers by the officials, by the majority and even by the family members just for praying for peace, and fairly being blamed by the victims and the whole thinking world. Still, the history of humanity is going around in circles, so there are ways to live through similar types of trauma. Ali shows his readers the direction. But is cultural creativity the only way out of trauma? And would it be enough to heal our sad world?

Dasha S. — Saint Petersburg, Russia

Please send letters for the winter issue to letters@thehappyreader.com

Everyone needs to read *The Odyssey* at least once in their lives, so why not devour the sprawling Greek epic in time for the next issue of *The Happy Reader*?

SAIL THROUGH THE ODYSSEY

Some books are just books. Others are the context we live in. Homer's *The Odyssey*, here announced as Book of the Season for the next *Happy Reader*, was probably written in ancient Greece in the seventh or eighth century BCE. Or perhaps it was the ninth, or the tenth, or the eleventh. No one knows. Equally, no one knows whether Homer was really a blind man living on the island of Chios surrounded by reciters of his poetry, as traditional accounts have it, or whether *The Odyssey* and its sister epic, the *Iliad*, which are the only evidence of Homer's existence, were in fact organically arising amalgams of orally transmitted legends. Was Homer himself as much of a myth as the giant one-eyed Cyclops? We don't know.

What we do know is that this proto-road movie was incalculably important to Greek, therefore Roman, therefore Western culture. Partly this is because it's just so fantastical and rich, a stormy cauldron of monsters, gods, nymphs and witches. The cliffhangers are thrilling, the twists nail-biting. It's a page-turner that looks impressive on the bus. *The Odyssey* has a special relationship with this magazine's beloved publisher, having been, in 1946, the first book to be published under the Penguin Classics imprint, a fitting start to a list taking in so many books with a palpable impact on the world beyond.

Winter's *Happy Reader* will be published in December. As you read, or reread, *The Odyssey*, it's recommended you take notes. Send the best to letters@thehappyreader.com. In the meantime, you may also enjoy the editor-in-chief's newsletter, *Happy Readings*. Receive it for free each month by subscribing at thehappyreader.com/newsletter.

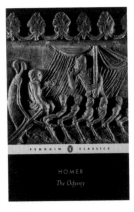

Jacket for *The Odyssey* by Homer.